Praise for *21 Ways to Run a* [barcode: I0065575]

"At last! Someone finally wrote an easy-[...] book that helps me stay stress free while running my bus[...] Whether you are a new or seasoned entrepreneur, this is one powerful book that immediately shows you amazing techniques to use right now. I found myself implementing the first chapter within minutes! It's THAT good!"

—Martha Giffen, best-selling author of *Be Social Be Rich,* MarthaGiffen.com

"There's a reason the book is called 21 Ways and not 21 Tips. Dr. Daisy doesn't leave you hanging with one-liners. She digs in and shares the how-to's of de-stressing yourself and making your business thrive. It's concise, informative, and motivational. (Way 15 on page 68 is one of my fav Way's! Great advice.)"

—Yvonne Lyon

"Business owners need Dr. Daisy Sutherland's book, *21 Ways to Run a Stress-Free Business*. Every entrepreneur and executive I work with has come with issues that create stress. The basic techniques Dr. Sutherland describes are simple to implement and sure to alleviate the tensions we tolerate. When we neglect to take care of ourselves, our work suffers. Create stress-less strategies and you'll create a better business."

—Dr. Lisa Van Allen, "The Business Doctor," VanAllenCoaching.com

"*21 Ways to Run a Stress-Free Business* is a must read for anyone desiring to start a business. It is well written, simple, practical, easy to read and just downright good. Dr. Daisy has taken the "fluff" out of the book, thus the 97 pages, and has included excellent references with corresponding QR codes. This is a book that should be read annually to maintain balance in your life."

—Carolyn Garnett Gray, Connecting Hearts Coaching
ConnectingHeartsCoaching.com

"Simple, direct and effective, the way a book on stress relief should be! It confirmed somethings that are already working for me, and gave me new practical exercises to reduce stress and grow my business. It is as much a business book as a stress relief book."

—Les Kletke, author/writing coach, GlobalGhostwriter.com

"This book offered many ways to help someone relax and have a 'clutter free' mind. The tips given in the book could be applied to anyone and is a good read for anyone who may feel overwhelmed. Of course, anyone with a business could benefit as well. It offered simple and cost-free ways to enjoy your surroundings and stay metally and physically fit as well."

—Vonna R. Weekly, author of *Baltimore Bites*

"*21 Ways to Run a Stress-Free Business* is a small read with a big impact. Daisy Sutherland shares with us, simple, time honored tips that can each reduce the level of stress we experience in our very demanding business lives. Having these strategies together in one easily accessible place is invaluable. I read this in one sitting and then implemented two of the Ways over the weekend. I saw an immediate effect on my ability to focus, and felt more relaxed and energized."

—Staci Clarke, national speaker, entrepreneur & Chief Networking Officer/V.P. Operations NetworkingEventFinders.com

"I wish I had this guide in the early days of my entrepreneurial journey. As a business owner, your most valuable assets are you, your time and your energy. Dr. Daisy Sutherland has created a wonderful road map for honoring your true priorities and harnessing your own self-care so that you can thrive and succeed in today's fast paced business climate. I am recommending this to all my friends and clients."

—Jill Koenig, author, self-made millionaire, GoalGuru.com

"In *21 Ways to Run a Stress-Free Business*, Dr. Daisy Sutherland offers simplistic ways to manage a business without being heavy-burdened by stress. In today's tough economy, most people are desperate to making ends meet which often times lead to incredible stress and frustration. As a Business Coach, sadly, I see business owners on the verge of giving up their entrepreneurial dreams due to said stress and frustration. Within the pages of this book, Dr. Sutherland offers easy-to-implement and practical advice to assist the reader in overcoming stress in both business and life. I highly recommend this book."

—Kelli Claypool, The Unconventional Business Coach & CEO of the Small Business Learning Institute www.BusinessAndLearning.com

"Short, easy-to-read, and filled with 21 easy ways to reduce stress! I began practicing the first three techniques as I was reading and they work! This book is a 'must' for entrepreneurs."

—Kim Gebron, The Nellie B Company, LLC

21 Ways to Run a Stress-Free Business

21 WAYS

to **run** a

stress-free
business

Dr. Daisy Sutherland

Discover BOOKS™
an Imprint of Imagine! Books™

High Point, North Carolina

21 Ways™ Series, Book 7

Published by Discover! Books™
an Imprint of Imagine! Books™
PO Box 16268, High Point, NC 27261
contact@artsimagine.com

Imagine! Books™ is an enterprise of Imagine! Studios™
Visit us online at www.artsimagine.com

Copyright © 2012 Dr. Daisy Sutherland
Cover Design © 2012 Imagine! Studios™
Illustrations by Drawperfect, purchased at istockphoto.com

All rights reserved. No part of this publication may be reproduced
or transmitted in any form or by any means, including informational
storage and retrieval systems, without permission in writing from
the copyright holder, except for brief quotations in a review.

ISBN 13: 978-1-937944-08-7

First Discover! Books™ printing, July 2012

Dedication

For my husband and soul mate David,
who supports and loves me.

You are my true inspiration.

Acknowledgements

A special thank you to

My family, who keep me motivated and grounded, all at the same time. My loving husband, David, for his unstoppable support and love, and for being a wonderful business partner.

My heavenly father, who watches over me, guides me, and shows unconditional love to me.

Introduction

It is quite common for a business owner to be stressed. The responsibilities that come with the title of business owner and entrepreneur are many, but they don't have to include being overtaken by stress. I created this book for you in the hope that these tips will reduce your stress or stop it in its tracks.

Stress is a very real part of life, and it's false to think you can live entirely without it. After all, some people love the energy that stress brings in reasonable doses. Stress, however, is manageable, and once you recognize the signs and symptoms you will be better prepared to handle them and not allow them to overwhelm you.

One of my goals as a business owner is to wake up each morning excited to work and touch people's lives. This is only possible if I'm able to successfully manage the situations that may cause stress. In this little book I share tips designed to help you manage and reduce stress levels. More importantly, these tips will help you identify situations and people that may produce needless stress before the fact. Once you identify the signals you will be able to stop stress before it takes over your mind and begins to affect every aspect of your business and your life.

So, sit down, put your feet up, and take in the tips shared in this book. Not only will you discover ways to reduce your stress, but you will also receive glimpses of ways that your business can begin to flourish as you never dreamed it could. Enjoy!

Dr. Daisy Sutherland

Take a Cleansing Breath

Oh sure, you may be thinking, "How will learning how to breathe reduce my stress?" However, you may be surprised at how your breathing can actually help. When you are stressed or feeling pressured, the first thing that will happen is that your entire body will stiffen and tighten up. When your body is tight, the last thing on your mind is to breathe, so naturally you will begin to feel stressed.

Here's a great example to prove you are not breathing correctly. Have you ever watched a baby breathe? If you look closely, you will notice that their chests move, their bellies pop and the front of their little bodies ride like a raft on waves. The pelvis will rock and the legs come apart and will come back together to complete the breath. They are actually exhibiting full body breathing. The way we as adults should breathe is by having our bellies pop out on the inhale and again at the end of the exhale. Now do we usually breathe this way? The answer is easy—no! As we get older, our breathing tends to become more shallow—in the chest instead of the abdomen or belly. We also have a bad habit of holding our breath for seconds at a time, sometimes up to 100 times per day. Many times you won't realize you are doing this, which is why you must learn to focus.

Instead of tensing up when a stressful situation arises, take a deep breath in through your nose and then slowly release it through your mouth. You will notice that it will probably take more than just one deep breath before you begin to calm down, but the deep breathing will truly work. These deep breaths are what I call, "cleansing breaths." Cleansing breaths will bring in clean air and help you cleanse your body and mind by releasing the negativity you are housing. This negativity enhances your stress, which is what you are trying to keep at bay.

Let's face it, stress comes in all shapes and forms, but learning how to cope and handle it is what will keep you sane. Will you be able to completely eliminate stress? Probably not, and I would be lying if I gave you false promises, so I won't. However, you can learn to control how a stressful situation will affect your thought process. Focusing on breathing with your entire body can dramatically change the way you approach these inevitable roadblocks in your life.

If possible, the next time you feel your stress level rise, step away from the situation and focus on your breathing. It can take a mere five minutes to sit in a comfortable chair and practice your breathing. If you can't get away, take a moment to collect your thoughts, breathe, and proceed. You will be truly amazed at what a cleansing breath will do for your mindset. Your goal is to reduce your overall stress, so start by breathing correctly.

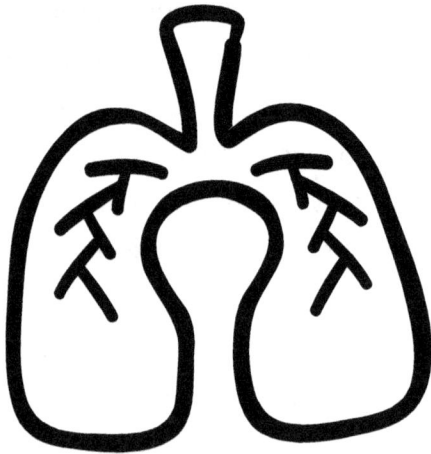

WAY 2

Make Time to Stretch

You will be amazed how stretching your muscles and spine will actually relieve your stress. Just as breathing helps to eliminate the stress housed in your body, stretching works wonders to release pent-up tension.

Think about it for a second. When you are faced with a stressful situation, such as seeing your bills pile up while collectors are calling or facing a huge project without the time or resources to tackle it all, your muscles will often begin to tighten. When this happens, lots of things begin to occur in your body. You get fuzzy thoughts because your head will start to ache, and you often won't be able to move or walk easily. Your sleep may even be interrupted.

It's important to get up and move your body and muscles from a fixed position. What's a fixed position? If you find yourself sitting for more than thirty minutes at a time, that's a fixed position. Not only are you sitting, but you also may be working on the computer or bent over your desk. These are not good positions to be in for an extended period of time. It's important to take a few minutes to get up. Move your legs, toes, arms—yes, your entire body.

Stretching your whole body will help to release the stress you are placing on your bones and muscles. Make a habit of getting up to move, get a drink, or go to the bathroom. Your body needs a change of position and your mind also needs a break. To ensure that you are moving and not staying in a fixed position, try using a timer. A simple egg timer will work or you can use your phone or set a timer on your computer. Whatever you decide to use, be sure to set it to go off thirty minutes after you initially sit down. You will be amazed how much work you can get accomplished in thirty minutes when you know a break is coming. When you take that break, you come back more focused and determined to get the project accomplished.

Some ways to get your muscles moving are walking, jumping, twisting, or simply pushing against a wall. What do I mean by pushing against a wall? When you are in a fixed position, your muscles will get tensed and need invigorating. Practice pushing on a wall, with your hands placed flat against the wall, and both your hands and feet shoulder-width apart. Using your body weight, push against the wall and release—similar to a push-up. Not only will you find you are more relaxed and less stressed, you will be actually working out the muscles that have been tensed.

Get up and stretch your body, even if you look silly. It's better to look silly and feel relaxed than to be tensed, stressed, and miserable. You will find yourself completing your tasks more quickly and you will be motivated to do more.

3

Get Moving

In addition to stretching your muscles, you can also battle stress by moving. No—not relocating your home or business! The moving I'm referring to is moving your body. It's amazing what actually moving your body can do to aid in relieving your stress. It's also good for your overall health.

Walking is the best type of basic moving activity. Walking doesn't cost a dime and can be beneficial to your health in general. It's important and fairly easy to schedule some walking time into your daily routine. Start by simply getting out of bed and walking to the bathroom. Then of course you must walk to get ready for the day. If you work at home, then make sure to schedule walking time throughout your day. If you work outside of the home, choose a parking spot that is far away from the entrance and take the stairs instead of the elevator.

Moving your body will stimulate your brain and reduce your stress levels. But don't stop at walking. How about playing some lively music and dancing? Yes, dancing is a great way to relieve your stress and get your body moving. If you have a video game system, put in a dance game like *Just Dance* (my family's favorite) and free yourself to be silly. If you incorporate this practice into your daily routine, you'll soon find your stress melting away.

As you're moving, focus on your body and try not to think of other things. Analyzing your actions will simply compound your stress level. Instead, make moving your body a game. Count the number of steps it takes to get to your location. Focus on moving not only your legs, but your arms as well. Try rolling your shoulders to the back and front to release the tension that tends to build in that area.

Most importantly, walk outside as much as you can. Fresh air is essential to your overall health and well-being. It is also a way for you to escape stressors that may be indoors. When you're outside, take note of all that is around you. If you live in the city, notice the cars, lights, buildings, and people. If you live in a suburb or the country, focus on the trees, birds, sky, and the sounds around you. The main purpose of going outside and getting moving is to not only to increase your daily activity, but also to release the stressors that surround you.

Nothing will beat stress better than moving your body. If walking or dancing is not enough, then perhaps running or jogging may help. Of course if you are new to this activity, be sure to take it slowly at first and work your way up to a more challenging pace. If running is not your style, consider taking an aerobics or spinning class at a local gym. As long as you are moving, you working off what is stressing you and you will be getting the physical activity your body needs as well.

4

Write Your Stress Away

Don't shake your head; this actually works. There are times when you will need to motivate yourself, because quite frankly others will not know how. Whether you write affirming notes to yourself or banish negative thoughts to paper and then throw them away, writing things out can be both therapeutic and cathartic.

If you want to surprise yourself with good words on a hard day, here's an exercise that may seem silly or simple, but which actually works. When you are feeling great, take that opportunity to write down everything you accomplished and how it made you feel. Be sure to add praises you received from others on your accomplishments as well.

Write a few of these notes and schedule them to go out via e-mail at least twice a month. (Use an e-mail autoresponder system like AWeber.) There will be moments throughout each month that are very stressful. Perhaps you have a deadline that you believe is not humanly possible to complete. Or your car just broke down and you don't have the money for repairs. The list can go on depending on your situation. Receiving uplifting notes in your inbox will not only make you step back and appreciate what you have, but it will also snap you back to reality.

When you are going through stressful moments, it's quite normal to only think of doom and gloom. The problems in your life seem to escalate and you have a sense of drowning in quicksand. Sometimes all it takes is an optimistic word that you wrote down to shed some light on your present situation.

If e-mails are not your thing or you simply can't bring yourself to do it, consider purchasing some cards and sending them to yourself. Yes, purchase blank cards, write down encouraging words and mail them to yourself. It may sound odd, but you will certainly be pleased to not only receive mail but also to open up the card to encouraging words that you wrote to yourself. Use a service like SendOutCards to automate this process and schedule surprise notes for yourself through the mail.

The entire purpose of this exercise is to make you aware that you will have good and bad days. The hope is that the good days will outweigh the bad days and your stress will be much more manageable.

If you'd prefer to try a more cathartic method, another way to use writing to deal with stress is to write out your negative thoughts. This practice will help you to write out your feelings and emotions rather than housing them within you, which can lead to stress, headaches, bad moods, sleepless nights, and even illness. The goal is to release all the negative thoughts and allow yourself to truly enjoy life. A great way to finally release and purge your negative thoughts is to tear up the paper or note to self and discard. I have gone a bit further and suggested to some people who may house their negative thoughts to burn the paper. This is thought of as closure and is a finite way of letting go of the negative thoughts.

Go ahead and write out how great you look, how well you're doing your budgeting, how you are keeping up with the demands of work and life in general. You will certainly welcome those fun and positive words and who knows you better than *you*? You can write crazy stuff, positive stuff, or words that will kick you back into action. Pick up your pen today!

Resources in this Way:

AWeber

SendOutCards

WAY 5

Reduce the Clutter

You will be surprised how reducing clutter will help reduce your stress. Of course, keeping your workspace in order will make your life much easier, but that's not the only clutter I'm referring to. The clutter in your mind must be taken care of as well in order to focus on your task at hand.

One of the ways to reduce the clutter in your mind is by writing out your to-do list. Putting it on paper is important to get it out of your mind and begin to map out a plan getting things done. However, just because you write your list down doesn't mean you have to complete all of the tasks in one day. What you must get in the practice of doing is writing down everything you want to accomplish, in your business and in your life. Do you want to create a new service or product? Perhaps you'd like to manage your working hours in order to spend more time with your family? Is there a goal you want to reach? The goals can be monetary or simply one for more time. It's wise to determine your goals in order to reduce not only physical clutter, but also the clutter in your mind.

Once you determine what your plans are, it's important to get them out of your mind and place them on a board or note pad that you can refer to often. You will soon notice that your stress levels will be dramatically reduced simply because you've made your goals more concrete by writing them down. Of course you don't want to stress yourself even more with your list. Again, I must repeat myself here because it's important to note that all the activities on your list do not have to be accomplished in one day, or even one week.

The items on the list should consist not only of items that you can easily accomplish in one day but also of tasks that can be worked on weekly and monthly. See Way 9 for more on managing your list.

You can also accomplish reduction of clutter if you learn to incorporate delegation into your processes. Who says you must do it all alone? This may be one of the biggest reasons you are stressed! Assigning projects to others is important, wise, and essential to keeping your sanity. Breaking down your list into bite-sized pieces will make it easier to assign these tasks to others. Of course, you must learn to trust others and let control go on those items you delegate, or you run the risk of making more stress for yourself. More on this in Way 6.

If there is a certain method required to complete a task you are assigning, make sure to explain it thoroughly and, if possible, show them how it is done and then let it go. You will notice that your clutter will decrease dramatically when you allow others to help you. As difficult as it is to let go, it is extremely essential to the success of your business and the reduction of stress. So, work on de-cluttering your workspace and your mind. This may take some time at first, but the time and energy you save later will be well worth it in the end.

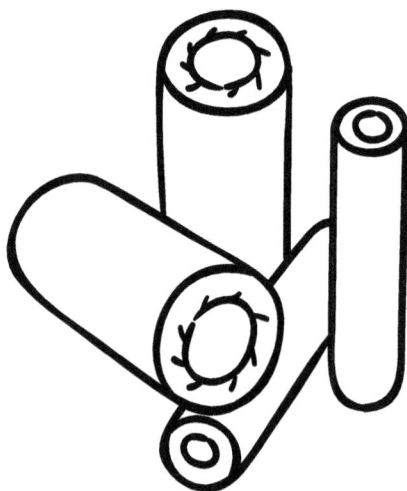

WAY 6

Know Your Limits

Whether your business is online or offline it is very important to not only know but to truly understand your limits. Too often many business owners will go beyond their limitations and of course they will be faced with the inevitable—*stress!*

Knowing your limitations will certainly help in reducing your stress levels, and it can also help improve your overall health. When you are stressed your immune system is compromised. Your immune system is what helps you fight off illness, and when you are stressed your body will be more susceptible. Once you face the fact that you cannot do it all yourself, healing of your immune system will begin. It's important to give your body rest so that it can heal and prepare for the work you need to accomplish.

So stave off those negative effects by sharing the work of your business. If you can't do the marketing for your business, then hire some-one who can help. If you can't afford to hire someone then you need to re-evaluate your budget. In order for your business to be suc-cessful and your stress levels to be reduced, you must share your business with others. Remember the "if you build it, they will come" philosophy only works in the movies. Of course you must work diligently in all ways possible to increase the revenue of your busi-ness, but this does not mean that all the tasks involved must rest on your shoulders. Learn to delegate.

Simple steps in recognizing your limitations and learning to share the load:

✓ Assess the project and what it entails

✓ Break it up into parts, identifying what you must do and what can be done by others

✓ Delegate tasks that can be done by others to others

✓ Set a realistic time frame for the completion of each portion of the project

✓ Once complete, review what worked, what didn't work, and move on to the next task

Consider taking a different approach to your business and your duties. Don't think of this assessment as a chore. Instead, be enthusiastic about what you do. It may seem redundant, but you have to get the job or project done, so you might as well make the process fun. And part of the fun is involving others, allowing them to grow in confidence and competence.

When you take this different approach to a project, you won't feel stressed and forced to do something you don't want to or simply can't accomplish. There's always someone out there who can do the job or project efficiently and in perhaps even in less time. Stop stressing over something you will have to learn first in order to complete and find someone who already knows how to do it.

Save yourself some precious time by outsourcing or finding someone within your company who can do a project or portions of a project. This is a major part of business and it is what separates the successful business owners from the ones that are just scraping by. You want to be successful—who doesn't? So start implementing what successful business people already do: Know your limitations and delegate.

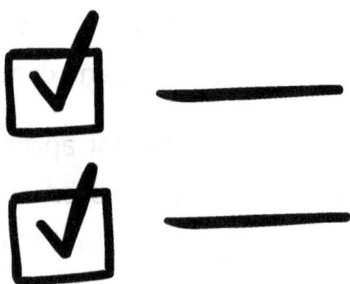

WAY 7

Get Creative with Your Business

Having your own business can be very fulfilling, but it can also become quite stressful. Some of the things that can bring on this stress may range from illness, lack of help, disorganization, and lack of money. In fact, not bringing in enough money to stay afloat can be one of the biggest stressors for any business.

Aside from wishing for more money, which honestly doesn't really work, there are other ways to increase your business revenue. One of the first things to look at is your expense budget. Perhaps there are areas you can do without in order to save some money. Do you really need to go out to lunch every day? Bringing in a bagged lunch two or three times a week will certainly save you money, but that is merely one example. Consider joining loyalty programs at the stores you frequent. Many stores have programs that entitle you to purchase items at wholesale prices and many will not include tax if you provide the appropriate paperwork.

Say you've gone through your budget and streamlined your expenses, but you still aren't making enough money and your stress level is rising. That is the time to consider getting creative in another way: creating new products or services, or grouping together some existing items to create a different offer or service. The possibilities are endless.

Many consumers are willing to try a new service if you have a free trial period that automatically charges starting the following month, or an introductory "early bird" price.

Is there something you already offer that you can consider adding on a trial period? Do you have products or services you can combine into a package and then offer an introductory "early bird" price?

Another creative option is to refresh your business's look. If you have an online business, perhaps you can change the graphics or look of your products or services. Sometimes simply changing the wording or graphics on your website will help bring in more traffic.

Additionally, since advertising both online and offline is essential to the growth of any business, consider creating some advertising methods, including some that don't cost money but can engage your target clients and customers in an interactive way, for example social media outlets such as Twitter, Facebook, or Pinterest.

As you can tell, the list can go on and on. The fact that your stress may be increased because of a lack of revenue should not make you run and hide. Instead, it's time for brainstorming with other business owners or people you trust to help you determine ways to bring in more money and reduce your existing costs. Be open to suggestions and ideas from others.

Let's face it, stress is not fun and no one wants to work or do business with a stressed individual. Not only will you scare people away, but they could also tell their friends. So, please, take a deep breath and relax. Be creative with your budget, services and products, and advertising in order to increase your customer base. Once you set your mind to this, don't allow negativity or doubt to set in. Say to yourself, "I can do this," and *believe* those words. Your stress will be reduced and your business will begin to succeed!

WAY 8

Connect with Others

If you are an entrepreneur, then you understand how lonely it can get. Connecting with other people may not be as easy as it sounds. However, it is easy if you connect with like-minded people. Who says that just because you are the boss you must sit in your office alone?

Haven't you ever felt like brainstorming with someone, perhaps bouncing ideas or simply talking about all the ideas spinning in your head? It is wonderful to have supportive family members and friends, but many of them don't understand how the mind of an entrepreneur works. It is not like the mind of one who works in the corporate world or works for someone else. An entrepreneur's mind never stops and is always coming up with ideas and ways to improve business and sales.

Stress is inevitable in the world of an entrepreneur and business owner. However, you do not have to deal with the stress alone. Connect with others who have the same thought processes as you.

Some places where you can find like-minded individuals:

Social Media

There are many business people who turn to the online world to connect with like-minded individuals. The most popular social media platforms right now are Facebook, LinkedIn, and Google +. These connections can lead to business partnerships and collaborations both online and offline.

Online Communities

There are communities online for each given specialty or niche. Many entrepreneurs will connect in these communities online because they don't have to leave their place of business or home in order to network. Google a keyword for your niche, like "writing" and then the word "forum" or "community" and see what results you get. Before you join a community, it's important to research them. Be sure to ask several questions to determine if this is a group you want to be a part of.

There are several local businesses and clubs that also have an online presence for people who are unable to connect offline. A perfect example of such community is Working Women of Tampa Bay. This group has a great presence online as well as events within the community enabling working women to stay in touch and connect.

Local Business Communities

Although the online world is wonderful, it is essential to connect with like-minded people in the "real world" as well. Not only are connections essential, but speaking to someone face-to-face and building relationships in that manner will also help build your business. Check out local networking groups such as the Chamber of Commerce, Rotary Clubs, Toastmasters, BNI, and BBB in your area, There are many local clubs that will meet on a monthly basis in order to build solid relationships with local business owners. This is a wonderful group to consider visiting and connecting with the other like-minded business owners.

The most important thing to remember in business is that *you are not alone.* This feeling of loneliness can certainly bring on unnecessary stress, so when you feel the loneliness coming, turn to the above places, or others, for help.

Resources in this Way:

 Facebook.com

LinkedIn.com

Plus.Google.com

Rotary.org

Toastmasters.org

WorkingWomenofTampaBay.com

BNI.com

ChamberOfCommerce.com

BBB.org

WAY 9

Choose Five Things

Take a look at your to-do list (or create one in Way 5). Do you have a never-ending list? This may be the biggest reason why you are stressed. As a business owner, you understand what must be accomplished daily in order to keep your business running. However, this list may get a little out of hand and therefore create unnecessary stress.

Instead of a long list, consider choosing five things you must do each day and stick to those five. Be sure to write these items down and most importantly cross them off of your list once you have completed the tasks.

Why five? Honestly, there is no rhyme or reason to choosing that particular number other than the fact that this is a number that can often be easily accomplished. Once your to-do list is completed for the day, you are able to focus on the following day's list and, most important, celebrate your accomplishments.

Of course, the five tasks on your list must be attainable. Don't fall into the trap of making the tasks so involved that you are back where you began with needless stress.

Here are the simple steps to get your five things done:

✓ Assess the your list and determine what five things you need to accomplish.

✓ Set a timer for fifteen to twenty minutes.

✓ Use earplugs or headphones. They help you focus and avoid distractions.

✓ Get up after your timer goes off, stretch, and refresh your mind.

✓ Cross each item off your list when it's completed and celebrate that accomplishment.

✓ Tackle the next item.

This is a pattern that has proven to work with many business owners. There is another system called the Pomodoro Technique, which focuses time in 25-minute increments with five minute breaks in between. Instead of allowing stress to take over, it is wise to look at different systems that have worked with other successful business owners and choose one that will work for you. Consider the system above and start with five of the most important tasks. Once you successfully accomplish five, you may then add more to your list for that day. Just don't let the list grow too long.

Resources in this Way:

 Pomodorotechnique.com

WAY 10

Get Fresh Air

Getting a little fresh air sounds easy enough, but you'll be shocked to know how often you probably disregard this important tip.

As a business owner it is very easy to get preoccupied with all the work that occurs indoors. Many entrepreneurs, if not most, will step into their office and not see daylight until the next day. This is especially true of those who work from home. This is not healthy and can certainly bring on unwanted and needless stress and anxiety.

It's important to step outside and enjoy some fresh air. Enjoying some fresh air will help to clear your mind and re-focus your energy to more productive projects. Not only is it great for your body, but your mind will thank you as well.

How do you incorporate fresh air into your daily routine? Here are some tips:

Schedule time in your planner or calendar each day to go outside.

Go outside for lunch instead of eating at your desk.

Set a timer for fifteen minutes and use that time to go outside and enjoy the sunshine

Schedule your errands during your lunch hour—this will force you to leave the office

You may notice that these tips are not difficult; however, avoiding, managing, and reducing stress requires effort on your part. It would be easy if we could simply delegate our stress to someone else, but we all know that is not possible. And, of course, that wouldn't be very nice. Instead, being aware of what may cause the stress is the first step to reducing it.

If you find yourself going in a million and one directions, this is a major indication that you must step away from your current task and step outside. Try it; you will see it truly works!

11

Plan Your Work and Work Your Plan

As a business owner or entrepreneur, it is important to try to keep one step ahead your competition. One way to do this is by planning ahead. This process of planning ahead will not only help you achieve success in your business, but it will lessen your stress levels as well.

As a new entrepreneur you may have had to create a business plan for your investors or lender. Regardless of the reason for creating one, every business should have a business plan in place, which formally states the business's goals, the reasons why these goals are attainable, and the plan for reaching the set goals.

Once this plan is written, you can use it to "plan ahead," which refers to a much more immediate time frame than your business plan. When planning ahead, you must take into consideration the weeks ahead as well as upcoming months and seasons.

Refer to your business plan often when doing your short-term planning, making adjustments to the master plan as needed. If one of your business goals is to obtain 100 new clients each month, you must have a plan in place to achieve this. Your business plan will address this goal by means of finance, human resources, and marketing, among other resources. You want to then break the goal down into manageable tasks and figure out the best way to work toward this goal in the short term as well as in the long term.

Consider having a large calendar where you can place all the month's activities and place it where it can be seen at a glance. Knowing your upcoming plans in advance will help you strategize your longer-term plans. It will also help you determine the cost involved, as well as the possible extra manpower needed to make your plans a success.

Here are some great simple tools to help you plan ahead:

✓ A large visible calendar

✓ Colored markers or highlighters

✓ Journal or notebook to write out your ideas

✓ Easel with paper or whiteboard to write out your plans for your entire team to see

These are simple tools that are often forgotten in the life of a businessperson. Sure, electronic gadgets are also helpful, but only if you truly use them.

Many times having your plans written out on paper, a white board, or a pad on an easel is enough to boost your creativity and energy to move ahead in your business. You will find your stress levels dramatically reduced when you can easily see both your long-term and short-term plans and work toward achieving them every day.

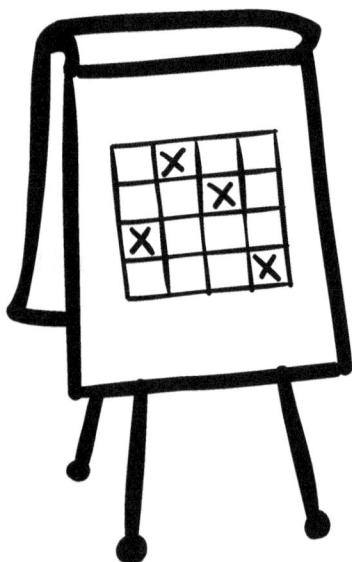

WAY 12

Know Your Client or Customer

This may be one of the most important Ways of all in this book. As a business owner, you can easily get preoccupied with marketing and establishing your business, all the time focusing primarily on yourself, but knowing your client or customer is truly essential to your success. Do you know your ideal client or customer?

Notice the question. It's not enough to know who your client is, but more importantly who your *ideal* client is. When you are able to determine who your *ideal* client is, then you can market and build your business accordingly. Not knowing who your *ideal* client is will have you running in circles trying to please everyone, and stress will inevitably appear.

Determine who you want to be of service to and then narrow it down further. Notice the word *narrow*. Narrowing down your ideal client will help you focus on the people who will benefit from what you have to offer and vice versa, which will in turn reduce your stress in your business. It's not enough to say your ideal clients are men or women—get more specific. Here are some questions to ask yourself to determine who your ideal client is:

✓ Male or female?

✓ Married or single?

✓ Older or younger? Specific age?

✓ With or without children?

✓ Level of education?

✓ Current occupation?

✓ Where do they live?

Of course these are merely the start of the questions you must ask yourself. Once you determine what categories your ideal client fits in, you will then understand what is needed to service your clients. Most of the stress that many business people encounter is the feeling that they "need" to help or service everyone.

Although it would be wonderful to service everyone, it is not humanly possible. Understanding this very important fact will help to lessen the stress you are placing upon yourself.

WAY 13

Organization Is the Key

Business owners must be organized or they will spend their days searching for things or wondering what they should be working on. It doesn't matter if you are in direct sales, a coach, a brick and mortar business owner, or one who owns a business online, organization is a key to reducing your stress.

There are many ways to be organized. Some organizational tips are geared to specific businesses while others are generic enough that any business owner can use them.

E-mail

E-mail is one of the most unorganized tasks that business owners have. They often receive so much junk e-mail that it can be stressful to simply click through and delete. Most e-mail programs have filters that you can set up that will help with junk e-mail. Take a little time to go through your junk e-mail and unsubscribe from newsletters or lists that are not directly related to your industry or that you've found you don't read anyway.

You should also create folders based on your needs that you can either move e-mails to or you can set up filters that will automatically move them to that folder. If you use filters you will need to set up a system that will remind you to check that folder often so you don't forget about something you need to do.

Computer files

Depending on the type of business you have, you may have a few or thousands of files on your computer. These can become a problem if you have too many, so it's a good idea to create folders for each customer or client or type of file you create. This will save you time searching for it later.

Paper copies

If you have copies of papers that you need to keep, consider using file folders to keep them nice, neat, and organized. Figure out a labeling system that works for your needs and create folders for each project—all your receipts, mail, and other papers you have messily stacked on your desk. To stay organized and feel less stress, you should file on at least a weekly basis. This will keep your stacks of paper to a minimum and it will take less time each time you file.

There are many different tips that you can use to create an organized business. Take a few minutes to look at your business and your office to see what you can do to organize things so you can work efficiently and effectively. You may also want to check out the book, *There's No Place Like Working from Home* by professional organizer, Elaine Quinn for great office organization tips and step-by-step plans. By starting with the steps listed above, you will feel great about working each day and you will increase the time you have to work on your business—not to mention the natural reduction of stress.

Resources in this Way:

 Book: *There's No Place Like Working from Home* by Elaine Quinn

WAY 14

Reduce Your Debt

Perhaps one of the most stressful issues every business owner may deal with is debt. Let's face it, when you own a business, you will spend. You may have heard the saying, "You have to spend money to make money"; however, this doesn't mean you have to go into extreme debt.

Instead of losing sleep over business debt, which will merely add to your stress, it is best to develop a plan and system for your business budget. Many individuals do not like to think about budgets because the word can carry the connotation of doing without, but it is essential to keep your business's doors open.

The budget tends to be manageable when done monthly as opposed to quarterly or longer. Consider the following tips:

✓ Keep a ledger of all expenses.

✓ Keep a ledger of all monies collected.

✓ Keep your business and personal accounts separate.

✓ Contact an accountant for tax deduction rules, and to file your business and personal taxes.

✓ Keep all your receipts.

✓ If you business involves travel, keep gas and car repair receipts.

It may seem overwhelming, but as a business owner it is essential to understand where your hard-earned money is spent. If you work a lot at the computer, I recommend the program Mvelopes from Crown Financial to assist you in tracking your spending and savings. You will be amazed how much money you'll save just by watching where it's going! If you are simply unable to manage your money, you are not alone. Hire someone you can trust to keep track of your finances.

Another thing to keep in mind is that cutting costs may be necessary in the establishment of a new business until a profit is evident. For example, if you are venturing into a new business, then consider purchasing used office equipment rather than new. Or purchase a more basic model until you can afford to upgrade. Look for ways to reuse and economize; just make sure that you have the resources you need to ensure the service you are offering to clients and customers is top quality.

Having your debt under control will reduce stress that may keep you up at night or unable to function properly. Something you must remember is that you are not alone (yes, I'm repeating myself on purpose). Your networks (see Way 8) will help you keep perspective.

Resources in this Way:

 Mvelopes

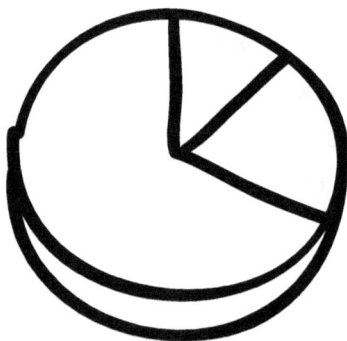

WAY 15

Stick to the Office Hours

Business owners often find it a bit difficult to stop working. There are times when an idea is born and there is no possible way you can consider stopping, but in order to control the stress that will inevitably present itself it is important to stick to a schedule and plan time to rest.

Whether your business is inside or outside the home, the business's hours must be set to where you have adequate time to service your customers, but also make time for you and your family and friends. Establishing the hours may be a difficult task, but once those are decided the next step is to abide by them.

Understanding that there must be a time for you to simply disconnect from your business is essential. There will be times when an idea will come up or an important phone call must be attended to, and those times are acceptable. What is not acceptable or healthy is working every waking moment. A successful and stress-free business owner is the one who understands his or her role in the business and, most importantly, understands when to set that role aside for other roles in his or her life.

A great way to remember how to shut down is to change your "hat." When you're working, you will obviously wear your business hat, but you must also learn to wear different hats. Learn to put on a different hat and be prepared to enjoy being a parent, spouse, athlete, reader, fisherman, painter, golfer, walker, volunteer, cook, or whatever non-work activities you like to do. Another word for this is to compartmentalize. This compartmentalization works in business and in life in general and will help to limit or manage the stress that naturally accompanies both business and day-to-day life.

If you work from home, it is best to set up a schedule and stick to it. Most importantly, make those around you aware of this schedule. You will not only stay focused, but you will also show those around you that you take your business seriously. Having a stress-free business is possible, but you must be willing to take the first step. Start with set hours to focus on business/work and then shut down when your schedule says it's time to go home. Sounds easy on paper; the trick will be applying it to your life.

It all begins with you learning how to separate business from family life. Not only will your business succeed, but your family life will also be much more enjoyable.

WAY 16

Take a Mental Vacation

Let's face it, as a busy entrepreneur or business owner you may not be in the position to take a vacation whenever you please, but that shouldn't stop you from taking a mental vacation. Some may call it daydreaming, but daydreaming is usually not very productive. A mental vacation will take you to the calm or sometimes the exciting place in your mind. This vacation will then refresh your mind to have the ability to focus on the task at hand.

This mental vacation can be as short as ten minutes or as long as thirty. The purpose of this exercise is to briefly take you away from the chaos that may surround you. When you close your eyes and visualize yourself with family, friends, or merely alone away from the office or home, you can focus more clearly. The point is to find a place in your mind that will help you relax and come back refreshed to finish the day.

Some business owners may take mental vacations daily and some don't visualize frequently. You will notice the one who can remove himself from the chaos and come back clear-minded and refreshed will have less stress surrounding him. Here are five easy steps to take a mental vacation:

Step 1

Find a quiet place in your office or home. If this is not possible, consider your vehicle or use earphones to muffle the outside noise.

Step 2

Get comfortable in your chair and close your eyes.

Step 3

Take several slow and shallow breaths in through your nose and out through your mouth.

Step 4

Now go to the place in your mind that will relax or invigorate you and focus on that place and see yourself there. Enjoy the surroundings.

Step 5

Remain there for several minutes. You may want to set a timer so you don't get lost.

Once you come back from your mental vacation, you will feel either relaxed and less stressed or invigorated and ready for a great rest of the day. When you find yourself spinning out of control (and those days will occur), give yourself a time-out and take a mental vacation. It truly works.

17

Choose the Right Foods

You may be wondering what choosing the right foods has to do with achieving a stress-free business. The answer is quite simple: Without proper nutrition your body will not function at its optimum, which will affect your mental and physical abilities. Choosing the right foods will help you focus and keep you energized to handle whatever stressful situations may arise in your business.

Your mother was right when she said the most important meal of the day is breakfast. A cup of coffee and a donut do not equate to a "real" breakfast. First, understanding why it is important will help you to accept the fact that your mother was right. Your body needs food to function at its optimum level. Think of food as fuel and your body as a machine. Without fuel the machine will not function. It may function sporadically, but eventually it will need fuel to keep it going. Your body works the same way. Now consider putting the machine to work for several hours without adequate and necessary fuel. It will break down.

When you are asleep your body is working on the reserves of the food you provided throughout the day. Unless you have figured out a way to eat while you are asleep, your body will need nutrition when it wakes up. Again, coffee does not equal food. Your body and your mind need food such as eggs, toast, bagels, smoothies, yogurt, oatmeal, or whatever your diet permits. Remember, this is the fuel that will help to energize your body and mind and prepare you for the day.

Once you have fueled your body and mind for the day with an early meal, it is also wise to have healthy snacks in your office. Keeping crackers, nuts, pretzels, fruits, and vegetables on hand will keep you from reaching for sugar-laden snacks. Remember, sugar may taste delicious, but if you ingest too much it will only give you temporary energy. Once the energy wears out, you will hit the wall fast and hard and stress will begin to creep in.

A healthy way to avoid stress is to choose healthy foods and snacks and include enough water in your daily diet. Not only will you be able to function more clearly, but your body and mind will also thank you.

Even if you do choose the "right" foods and include physical activity in your day, you may still suffer from various types of ailments such as a headache or allergies. Instead of rushing for over-the-counter medication consider natural alternatives.

WAY 18

Use O.P.M.

Nothing can be more stressful than money management. In any business money is a determining factor to how large you will grow. Some will argue that money is not necessary, that only passion and drive are needed to succeed. Although those components are major contributing factors to success in any business, money still remains No. 1 on the list.

Budgeting is essential in any business and household. Understanding what is needed to survive and what is essential to succeed in business will help to reduce your stress. But what happens when the money does not exist? That is where O.P.M. comes into play.

What exactly is O.P.M.? Quite simply it means "other people's money" and it is one of the first lessons taught in Business 101. If you have the opportunity to use "other people's money" to grow your business, why wouldn't you?

Now is the time to develop creative methods to implement this technique in your business. Crafting a proposal may seem stressful, but if you determine what your business may need financially to push it to the next level, it will be easier to ask people to help fund your dreams. Other people's money may be that of a close family member or friend or simply individuals who are seeking to invest their money in a business.

There are also grants and scholarships available and small business loans from the Small Business Administration (SBA.org) that can help as well. If you are working on a creative project you can use a website like Kickstarter. com or IndieGoGo.com to find sponsors and investors to fund your project.

You will need to create a business plan detailing how the money will be spent and a contract must be drawn up to protect all who are involved. Once you have your funds in hand, you are on your way to implementing your vision.

The point is to never feel that you can't succeed in business. If you firmly believe that your business is something that will help others, you should be able to convince others of the same. Accomplishing this will help your business grow and reduce the stress a lack of money can bring.

Resources in this Way:

SBA.org

Kickstarter.com

IndieGoGo.com

WAY 19

Affirmations

Do you walk into your office, whether at home or out of the home, with a smile? Are you thinking positively and ready for what the day will bring? If not, consider writing out and reading positive affirmations daily. If you are struggling with stress in your business and in your life in general, positive affirmations can work to lift your spirits.

Try implementing some positive thoughts and sayings into your daily routine. Affirmations work well in combination with meditation or quiet time. Instead of jumping out of bed and running for the shower every morning, spend your first fifteen minutes awake enjoying some quiet time with your affirmations. The process is simple and once you commit to doing it daily, it will become part of your morning and evening routines.

Find positive and thought-provoking quotations and print them out or write them in a notebook. Use these positive words to start your day. If you don't like reading or using words, consider calming music or photos. Implementing these into your daily routine will help you to approach the day in a more peaceful and calm mood and stress will not be present.

Here's an exercise you can implement into your morning rituals:

Step 1

Set alarm for fifteen minutes earlier than your usual time and turn off the alarm once it rings.

Step 2

Lie in bed and practice your breathing techniques from Way 1.

Step 3

Listen to soft and calming music as you focus on the beauty of yet another day and run your affirmations through your mind.

Step 4

Get up in fifteen minutes and continue with your morning routine.

Though you may find them silly at first, affirmations work and have been found to help many prominent individuals. Starting your day with affirmations and a positive frame of mind will help to reduce and manage the stressors that may arise during the day.

WAY 20

Have a Sense of Humor

Whether you've been in business for a while or you're trying to start one, the most important component of all is humor. Let's face it; there are days when nothing seems to go right. It can start with the alarm clock not sounding to burning a hole in your favorite slacks to a flat tire or worse. How do you approach those unforeseen circumstances? You have several choices ranging from screaming to crying, but the best choice is that of laughter.

Did you know people who laugh enjoy a healthier lifestyle? Not only will they be happier and healthier, but they will also be magnets to people. If you are a magnet to people you can be assured that your business will flourish. Think about it—who wants to do business with a grouchy or grumpy person?

Evidence suggests that laughter helps to reduce stress, increase your circulation, help you burn calories, boost your heart rate, and it's an all-around health promoter. How can you go wrong? One of the most effective ways to reduce stress, which can seriously damage your physical and emotional health, is to simply laugh. When you are stressed, your immune system can be compromised, making you susceptible to illness, infection, and disease (more on this in Way 6). As your stress is reduced you are ultimately happier, can sleep soundly, and enjoy better health. But, I'm sure you're wondering how laughter can help you burn calories.

Let's break down the science of laughter to help you better understand. When you laugh, you tend to move your entire body, including muscles that stretch and contract. Think back on how your belly ached from laughing so hard. How much easier is it to burn calories by simply laughing rather than by sweating in a gym? If I had to choose, you know which one I would prefer! Imagine: You can actually be healthier by simply adding laughter to your daily routine.

If you find it difficult to laugh, perhaps reading humorous writings will help. If that doesn't work, consider watching comedic movies or videos. Watch a funny movie, listen to your kid's jokes, look at life through different shades—you can do it. Surrounding yourself with happy and jolly people will also help to change your entire outlook on life. What better way to reduce the stress in your business than to simply laugh?

21

Acceptance

Understanding that stress is at times inevitable is the first step in acceptance. Too often people will try to avoid the fact that a situation is stressful and in fact will create more stress for themselves by worrying. Be aware of the situations, people, or circumstances that may bring on feelings of stress. When you are aware of such times, you will be able to better prepare your mind and body to deal with the stress coming your way. Accepting that many people around you are stressed will also help you know that you are not alone.

Simple techniques such as breathing (Way 1), taking naps, or simply talking to someone you trust will help in managing the stress your business or life in general will bring. Notice how I used the word "will." Your business *will* bring on stress, your life *will* have stressful moments, your employees *will* create more stress, and you must understand and accept the fact that stress is all around you.

Accepting that fact doesn't mean that you must and should give in to it. The entire purpose of accepting is to help you realize it exists and that you are capable of fighting it and keep it at bay. The sign of a successful and happy business owner is that he or she can handle stressful situations with a calm demeanor. Remember, your customers will not want to work with you or purchase from you if you are always stressed and seemingly overwhelmed by it. As much as you try to hide it, if you have not found a way to control it, your customers will notice.

The breathing technique shared in Way 1 will work wonders for you. Going outside and removing yourself from a stressful situation also works. Changing your perspective and finding other ways to handle stressful situations will be ultimate blessings in your business and life.

You are human and in your life many emotions will surface. The challenge is to calmly and assertively handle the situations as they arise with minimal anger or uneasiness. It will take practice, but remember that once you have identified your stressors, you will be able to prepare yourself and handle them appropriately.

As you learn to manage you own stress, you can even pass on what you know to others, including your employees. If you have employees that are showing signs of stress, the following tips will help:

✓ Frequently acknowledge employees for their extra work, and make them aware of how valuable they are and how much they are appreciated.

✓ Encourage employees to take short time-outs. Rather than ruminate and stew over their workloads, sometimes just taking short walk down the hallway can help them rejuvenate and refocus.

✓ Encourage employees to eat healthy (provide healthy food choices in the kitchen or cafeteria at work and acknowledge employees for making healthy dietary choices). Reward them for making healthy choices, since when we get stressed we tend to eat comfort foods, which are not healthful and may even actually add to our stress levels.

These tips also work for you! Soon you will notice your business is a less stressed environment and those involved will be happier and more productive.

Extra Tips

Rehydrate

Chances are you are drinking tea, coffee, juice, and perhaps energy drinks in your office all day long. However, those are not the fluids your body needs. Your body needs water. If you don't hydrate your body with water, your organs and body will suffer, and inevitably stress will enter. Most people need at least four to eight glasses of water each day. A great way to keep yourself hydrated is to have a water bottle on your desk at all times. This will ensure you are getting hydrated and reduce your stress in the process.

Power Nap

Taking a quick nap is a great way to recharge and re-energize your body and mind. A quick ten- to twenty-minute nap will also help to reduce needless stress. Set a timer for twenty minutes and let your mind relax. It's amazing how refreshed you will feel after a twenty-minute nap. If you find your business stressing you, be sure to schedule a few power naps—they will help.

Relaxation techniques

Explore and use relaxation methods such as the method laid out in Way 16. Other techniques include yoga, meditation, self-hypnosis, massage, or simply a breath of fresh air (see Way 10).

Share your worries

Talk to someone and share your feelings and concerns. Releasing these worries and concerns will help to reduce your stress. Keeping it all within you will merely create more stress and worry and will affect your overall health. See Way 8 for ways to connect with like-minded people who will understand what you share with them.

Encourage good time-management techniques

Planning for important activities, scheduling them in advance, following up with others, and keeping good records help people get things accomplished on time and realize their value. See Way 11 for step-by-step ways to plan your time and be sure to take time to make note of successes and projects accomplished.

Learn to say "no"

When your schedule is full, say "no" to activities you don't enjoy, unrealistic demands, and responsibilities that aren't yours. Doing this with tact and diplomacy takes some practice, but it will certainly help in reducing your stress.

Conclusion

After you read this book, my biggest hope is that you realize you are not alone. Stress is a huge factor in many business owners' lives and the first step to reducing it is knowing that it exists (see Way 21). Being aware of the factors that may bring on stress will help you run a successful, stress-free business.

The tips shared in this book will not only help you run a stress-free business, but they will help you create a stress-free life as well. Allowing others to help and truly enjoying your life are huge parts of your new stress-free journey. It will be difficult at first, but with practice and determination you will succeed.

Remember to breathe, stay active, choose healthy foods, smile, and get adequate amounts of sleep. Those tips sound simple enough, but you will be surprised how many will neglect one or all of them and find themselves spiraling out of control. Don't fall victim to stress—you too can be truly happy and successful.

Be happy and don't forget to smile!

About the Author

Dr. Daisy Sutherland is the Founder and CEO of Dr. Mommy Online. Her main mission and goal is to Inspire, Motivate & Encourage you to be the best you can be in health, wealth, and sanity!

She is a Doctor of Chiropractic, author, speaker, and radio personality, but most importantly she is a devoted wife and mom to five. She understands the trials of life and has overcome many, and because of this she is determined to help others through this wonderful journey we all call life!

She encourages you to not dwell on the past and allow it to form who you are today. Instead, you should learn from the past so you can become the greatness you were created to be. This is her motto and through her writings, audios, and speaking engagements, she continues her mission of inspiring, motivating, and encouraging others.

For more of what Dr. Mommy has to offer, visit her at DrMommyOnline.com

Do you feel lost?

Are you simply dragging through your week?

Do you have difficulty finishing projects?

Are the kids wearing you out?

Get FREE instant access to
Dr. Daisy's report

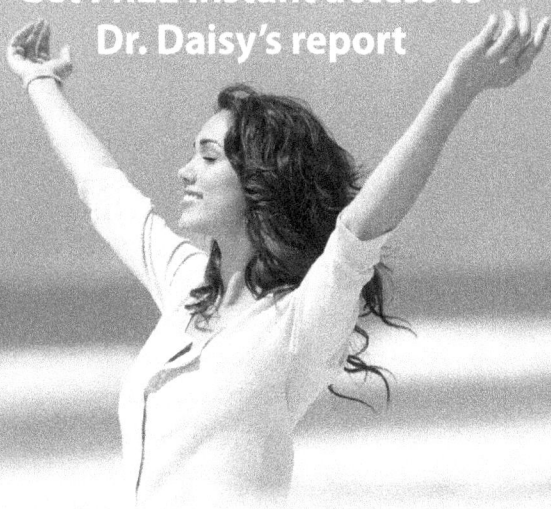

7 Simple Ways to Get Motivated

DrMommyOnline.com/motivated

97

Collect them all!

21 WAYS to **write &** **publish** your non-fiction **book**
Kristen Eckstein

21 WAYS to **powerfully** **network** your business
Kristen Eckstein

21 WAYS to enjoy a **stress-free** **holiday** season
Dr. Daisy Sutherland

21 WAYS to make **money** speaking
Felicia J. Slattery, M.A., M.Ad.Ed.

21 WAYS to **skyrocket** your **creativity**
Tony Laidig

21 WAYS to be a **kid** again & get **adult** **results**
Kristen Eckstein

21 WAYS to **run** a stress-free **business**
Dr. Daisy Sutherland

21 WAYS to **manage** the **stuff** that **sucks up** **your time**
Grace Marshall

Look for more *21 Ways*™ books at
21WaysBooks.com

www.ingramcontent.com/pod-product-compliance
Lightning Source LLC
Chambersburg PA
CBHW071718210326
41597CB00017B/2526

* 9 7 8 1 9 3 7 9 4 4 0 8 7 *